P9-CMX-952

Pursuit of
Happiness

WINSTON K. PENDLETON

Pursuit of Happiness

A Study of the Beatitudes

THE BETHANY PRESS
ST. LOUIS, MO.

COPYRIGHT © 1963 BY THE BETHANY PRESS

LIBRARY OF CONGRESS CATALOG CARD NUMBER 63-8824.

ISBN: 0-8272-2922-4

All Bible quotations in this volume are from the King James Version.

SIXTH PRINTING, 1974

Distributed by The G. R. Welch Company, Toronto, Ontario, Canada.

MANUFACTURED IN THE UNITED STATES OF AMERICA.

The Earl Nightingale program, "Our Changing World," is broadcast by more than 1,000 radio and television stations. The Bethany Press is proud to announce that *Pursuit of Happiness* now is available on tape cassettes, narrated by Mr. Nightingale for richer understanding through listening as well as reading. The cassettes, packaged with a copy of *Pursuit of Happiness*, are available from the Nightingale-Conant Corporation, 6677 N. Lincoln Ave., Chicago, Ill. 60645, or the Bethany Bookstore, 2640 Pine Blvd., P.O. Box 179, St. Louis, Mo. 63166.

Foreword

I met Win Pendleton at a business meeting in Orlando, Florida. Just meeting him is a memorable experience: there is about him a pervading aura of happiness, even exuberance. He is a person you remember meeting.

The next day at the airport, Win reappeared. Brimming with the same cheerfulness, he handed me a small book, saying, "Here's something to read on the flight home."

One of the qualities of "greatness" is that we come away from it—whether it's in a painting, music, drama, or work of any kind—changed for the better as persons. That is why so few works of art live on; why the great majority do not. This little book most assuredly qualifies as great. I read it with mounting interest and enthusiasm on the flight home. For the first time, I really understood—felt I had grasped the true meaning of what Jesus Christ said in his Beatitudes and what this great philosophy could mean in a person's life.

My business has always involved the spoken word. The human voice breathes life into words and when I read *Pursuit of Happiness*, I was consumed by the desire to read it aloud, to carry its great message to the ears of people everywhere. So I was delighted when Win and his publisher, Bethany Press, agreed to my narrating it.

As a rule, a person will read a book only once. It is difficult to understand fully and to make an integral part of our lives something that is read but once. Additionally, a book is usually read by only one or two adults in a family. In recorded form, great thoughts may be heard over and over again, until they become a part of us. They can be listened to while doing other things, while driving to and from work, while dressing or even working. And most importantly, they can be heard by all members of the family, even the children, even those children too young to read at all. And they change us for the better.

Read the book by all means! But listen to the recorded version of it too. Make sure that every member of your family hears this great piece of writing based on the words and wisdom of Jesus Christ.

EARL NIGHTINGALE

CONTENTS

PROLOGUE

A Search
and a Finding

This is the story of a search and a finding. I found a key—a key that unlocked a huge gate—and beyond that, a thousand doors. Some large, some small. Some opened easily. Others yielded only to pressure. Some led to halls, to other doors, and to more doors. Others opened into workrooms, or ended in closets.

A master key that unlocked treasure. More doors, more treasure.

But my search did not begin as an all-out effort. It was not that one morning I washed and dressed and tied my tie and said: "Today I begin the search. I'll keep at it until I find the answer." It wasn't like that. Not at all.

I had work to do, a family to support. Preoccupied with the matter of earning a living, I was not even conscious of when my search began. It began before I knew it. I simply found myself searching, and I searched when I did not know I was searching.

My search was at first quite vague. It was like trying to remember a name to match a face. You shrug it off and figure it will come to you. Or like selecting wallpaper. You choose a pattern, but you have the feeling you really wanted something else. Or like looking for a letter in the files. It haunts you. But you work on without it.

From this vagueness sprang awareness of a need to find some answers. I had no time to make the search. Yet, I needed answers, and believed they could be caught in passing. But answers somehow never came, and this fact bothered me.

I was bothered, but did not feel "disturbed." My friends may have thought otherwise. But I felt "normal," even as I groped for meaning. I had good days and bad days. The good days were all right, but rare. The bad days were quite bad, or so I thought.

I suppose, too, that everybody worries some about the things he should have said, or left unsaid. It is not unusual to look at yesterday with a shudder, to wish we had said "yes" instead of "no"—or "no" instead of "yes." I looked back a bit too often perhaps; and in my good moments I usually dreamed of better days ahead: what I would do, see, or have—tomorrow. But I seemed always to visualize tomorrows that never quite arrived.

In all of this, the pressures of the moment were upon me. The *now*, the *right now*.

"And for what?" I would ask. "Why the struggle? Why bother with being chairman of a committee to promote the cause of this or that? What does *this* or *that* mean anyway? Why the cheers and bows and clapping of hands? Why stay three weeks on a treadmill for one day at the beach? How are things related to each other? What is the fact of life that gives meaning to the *now?*"

Call it what you will—rat race, humdrum, see-saw, or something else—I rushed to work and home again. I ate and slept and worked. I worked and ate and slept.

I was busy, but bothered, and I would sometimes try to cancel out my irritations: "Why ask so many questions? You're better off than most. The bills are paid, usually, somehow. The house is warm, the car is new. You're able to walk. You live in a land of plenty. You are free to come and go as you please. You're richer than King Solomon ever dreamed of being. Count your blessings—your wife, the kids."

But such whistling in the dark only made the problem worse—because, I would say to myself, "If I really *am* so lucky, why do the clouds always roll in? Why do I shout and scream at those I love the most? Why is my stomach jumpy, my nights sleepless? Why do I have those dreary and tiresome hours?"

There I stood, hitchhiking through life; waiting for the long free ride; slightly cynical, but working hard; trying to save and get ahead, but somehow not showing much progress; reading some, watching television; happy one day, blue the next; loving wife and family, but grouchy and mean too; hoping for the best, but very anxious; confused and lost—maybe not lost, but at least wandering through the marshlands.

Then, I stumbled on a key. I didn't even know it *was* a key. But I picked it up anyway, examined it closely, tried to use it, and things gradually began to happen. Dark days turned bright, and the dirge turned into a symphony. Not all of the answers have come, but I know where to look. And the search—still in progress—is a joyous affair. It guarantees a full day of living, every day.

My search began to bear fruit only after my having to

fill in as a Sunday school teacher in our small church. I didn't really want the job. I didn't want to get involved. After all, church was a pleasant place to think and doze. Even the sermons—because I had never really listened to them—seemed geared to passive enjoyment. Besides, church was simply a habit with me. It meant status. Content to be a nonworker, I regarded the call to teach as a definite intrusion.

I accepted the job on a temporary basis. Just two Sundays, mind you, and that was final. But even though my frame of mind was decidedly temporary, I planned to do my best. I would approach the job as a newspaper man. I would probe unknown subjects by asking questions designed to unearth facts and essences. I would use Kipling's time-tested who-what-why-when-where-how technique. And in the habit of a steady hack, I would try to express my findings in simple terms.

This technique worked amazingly well. It proved that a journalist can discover facts of life as well as facts of political campaigns. This knowledge made me more enthusiastic, and the regular teacher somehow never came back. Two Sundays turned into three, three into four. Weeks turned into years, my temporary assignment gradually became permanent, and I was no longer reluctant. I was no longer a nonworker in our church.

My change in attitude came slowly, but it came. Full and complete. And with this change came knowledge of great truths and how they work. Answers at last—some obvious, some almost hidden, but answers, nevertheless.

Among my findings as a teacher, I prize none more highly than the Beatitudes of Jesus. I had known them, of course, for a long time. Urged by an older sister, I had memorized the Beatitudes even before starting to school.

But I knew only their words and not their real meanings. I found this to be true of so much I "knew" about Christianity.

I knew, for instance, the broad outline of the story, not the hidden meanings, not the essences. I knew a man named Jesus had lived and preached some two thousand years ago—that he was a Jew (although not much has been made of this fact); that he was born and raised in a small territory of the Roman Empire.

I knew that Jesus had some ideas about religion, ideas considered so radical they led to his execution; but that he arose from the dead, gave final instructions to his followers, and then disappeared.

I also knew that the followers of Jesus (I had never understood the difference between disciples and apostles) carried on the work; that the ideas of Jesus caught hold and spread; that they changed men's thinking; that they, in fact, changed the course of history.

Although Jesus did not write anything, I knew that his friends did—years later. The essence of his radical ideas was gathered into one document. We know this document today as the Sermon on the Mount. Found in Matthew 5—7, it has been called the most important writing ever given to man. The Beatitudes are included in the Sermon on the Mount.

I knew these facts. Yet, when it came time to teach half a dozen fellow churchgoers about this Sermon, I discovered that I didn't even understand its opening sentence. I was not at all sure what the Beatitudes meant, but I was determined to find out.

After much probing, I found that the Beatitudes point the way to hidden inner powers. If you will follow this way, it may also lead you to a new and fuller life. The

Beatitudes are rules for right living, uttered by the greatest person ever to walk the earth. Stated in Matthew 5:3-12, they are as follows:

Blessed are the poor in spirit: for theirs is the kingdom of heaven.

Blessed are they that mourn: for they shall be comforted.

Blessed are the meek: for they shall inherit the earth.

Blessed are they which do hunger and thirst after righteousness: for they shall be filled.

Blessed are the merciful: for they shall obtain mercy.

Blessed are the pure in heart: for they shall see God.

Blessed are the peacemakers: for they shall be called the children of God.

Blessed are they which are persecuted for righteousness' sake: for theirs is the kingdom of heaven.

Blessed are ye, when men shall revile you, and persecute you, and shall say all manner of evil against you falsely, for my sake.

Rejoice, and be exceeding glad: for great is your reward in heaven: for so persecuted they the prophets which were before you.

CHAPTER ONE

Problems:
Semantic and Otherwise

"Blessed are the poor in spirit . . .
for theirs is the kingdom of heaven."

I was stuck with a semantic problem before I started! What did Jesus mean by "blessed"?

I had heard the word many times, but mostly in church. I had never really used it, except in reference to a blessed event or perhaps to describe a person blessed with a long life. And the dictionary was not much help either, mainly because I could not decide which of its several definitions to use.

Did Jesus mean to describe a state of being which is holy, sacred, consecrated, full of great happiness, or one of eternal bliss? Which of these did he mean? Where was I to find the clue?

I decided the clue must be the people to whom Jesus spoke. His audience was evidently a huge crowd, a multitude. But where did these people come from, and why? Some were undoubtedly local, but there were others too, "from Decapolis, and from Jerusalem, and from Judaea, and from beyond the Jordan." (Matthew 4:25)

Why did they travel so far to see Jesus? What did they expect to hear? What did they desperately *want* to hear? The answer seems clear, because Jesus' fame had already spread. He had become known as a great healer.

Many of Jesus' hearers, then, suffered various physical and emotional ailments, and they had traveled many hard miles to be cured. Others had traveled with them—their friends and relatives. They had protected and comforted them along the way, and stayed beside them to help them through the crowd.

Another part of the multitude, undoubtedly, was simply curious. They were there, perhaps, just to see the show— to see what this teacher or preacher, or whatever he was, had to offer.

Aside from specific reasons for their presence, Jesus' hearers did have one thing in common whether they realized it or not. They all wanted better lives. Jesus knew this, because he knew human nature. He knew that his hearers—even those expecting merely to be entertained—craved answers to basic questions, questions still gnawing at men's souls today. These people wanted to know how to find a fuller life, how to find happiness, and they sought answers.

Jesus thus commanded attention right from the start by talking about something everybody wanted to hear, by listing a few short rules concerning how to be blessed, or happy. The Beatitudes are more than just a list. They are faith capsules uttered in poetic form. I wondered about this at first. I wondered why Jesus repeated the word "blessed" so often. Why didn't he just say, "Blessed are the following persons," and then list them?

Then I began to think about the long Hebrew tradition of poetic utterance, and the picture got clearer. Poetry, I am told, is actually older than prose. The most ancient writings in the Old Testament, as a matter of fact, are in poetic form. These writings suggest a time when great truths were preserved by word of mouth. It was natural for poetry to be the form in which these truths were transmitted, because poetry is easier to remember than prose.

Thus we find Jesus using two good techniques right at the beginning of his sermon. On the one hand, he talks about something the people want to hear, the great happiness principle. On the other, he summarizes this principle in a poetic capsule. This capsule can be carried home in the hearts and minds of his hearers.

What is this great happiness principle about which Jesus—in good Hebrew tradition—speaks so poetically? And is this principle relevant today?

As these questions ran through my mind, I realized the Beatitudes contradict values by which many persons live, and I wondered if they would really work, *for me*.

Before answering these questions, I had to understand more fully just what Jesus is talking about. I had learned that "blessed" must refer to a state of happiness; but I needed to analyze more words, more phrases—and so my search continued.

Stuck again! And for the same old semantic reason. What did Jesus mean by "poor in spirit"?

I wondered if this phrase meant the same as "poor in dollars." Was Jesus really saying that happy persons *lack* something? Was he saying that happiness depends upon a bankrupt spirit? Obviously not. Jesus had something else in mind. He was describing an attitude, a new approach to life.

In trying to discover this approach, I hit upon the idea of looking first at its opposite. What, I asked myself, would "rich in spirit" have meant to Jesus?

This approach helped—because the spirit (or attitude) of the rich in Jesus' day was recorded by New Testament writers. The rich—those who made wealth their sole object—were looked upon as arrogant, proud, overbearing, unjust, unmerciful, cruel, and domineering. The people who came to see and hear Jesus knew quite well what "rich in spirit" meant, and they could understand the opposite type of attitude.

The "poor in spirit," then, were humble folk. And humility is the first step toward a permanent state of happiness. Jesus referred to humility in the first Beatitude because this attitude is basic.

Pride, the opposite of humility, is dangerous because it is so subtle. It slips up on people. The child takes his first step, and then looks to see who is watching. He is bursting with a pride his parents and grandparents (especially grandparents) soon catch. They express their pride to all who will listen, and they encourage the child to be proud. His innocent pride turns into a habit and ceases to be innocent.

This illustration makes a point: It is only natural to encourage pride in a small child. But the child must eventually become a man and give up childish ways. Yet, the illustration is too simple, because it raises further questions it does not answer. A certain amount of pride is good, or at least unavoidable. Pride sometimes motivates good acts.

The answer seems to be that whether or not it promotes good acts, pride is unavoidable. Obviously, no man ever achieves perfection. We are finite beings, and as such, have a way of taking pride even in our own humility. This is another way of saying that man never escapes being sinful. In speaking of humble persons—those poor in spirit—Jesus, then, is talking about an ideal no man can fully achieve. Pride is always lurking in the shadows. It is always a threat to happiness. It is always ready to control a life.

Yet, pride does exist in degrees. It can be controlled, and man can at least *aim* in the direction of humility. Part of such an aim is being sensitive to the fact that pride is a sinful (or unhappy) element of life. Excessive pride exists certainly among those who are not sensitive to this fact. They are said to have the big head, and are sometimes described as being puffed-up, self-righteous, or snobbish. A politician, for instance, who begins to believe his own publicity material may be slave to a certain type of pride.

There are many types of pride, but some types are more familiar than others. Jesus had some stinging things to say about those who are proud of their opinions, the self-righteous. These persons close their minds completely to differing points of view and are downright uncharitable to those outside their circle. In effect, they seek to control God by saying magic words before him and by performing little rituals which dramatize the secret mystery which they alone behold.

A closely related type is pride in who we are: the pride sometimes expressed by "first families" who always remain aloof; the pride expressed by the country club set when they isolate themselves from the "ordinary" folks in the community; the pride expressed by certain leaders of state who boast that they are supermen.

Then there is pride simply in being right. This type

was once expressed rather humorously by a printer. He said: "I ain't never made but one grammatical error since I come to work here. I seen it when I done it, so I taken it back." We may smile at this printer, but in the eyes of God, we are very much like him. God undoubtedly smiles at us, especially when we make the preposterous claim that we are always right.

Among many other types is pride of achievement. Such pride makes men and women try to outdo their neighbors. This includes pride in clothes, homes, cars; pride in what we know, do, or have. This type of pride makes a fellow feel self-sufficient. It causes him to replace God with man-made replicas. It has resulted in an age of disillusionment and anxiety.

Despite these dismal thoughts, the Beatitudes of Jesus offer relief to those struggling for meaning in a world of apparent meaninglessness. The ideal model suggested by Jesus is the man who is, first of all, more humble than not—the modest fellow. The one who, forgetting himself, makes room for wonderful and exciting thoughts about other people and other things. Such a person is spared the mental isolation and anxiety that inevitably descends upon the self-centered.

The humble man is not worried about getting credit for things he does. He is not worried about his "rights." He does not interpret every remark as a veiled insult. He does not fear losing his status.

The humble man, then, is the happy man—and the great happiness principle behind the Beatitudes is now in sight. This principle is not to be equated with external values. Jesus did not believe, for instance, that happiness depends on wealth, prestige, cleverness, or superficial humor.

Jesus was talking about the happiness of a fuller and more abundant life, permanent happiness, an all-consuming feeling, an inner peace, a fullness of life—not just an occasional boost brought on by a snatch of external prosperity; but full-time happiness reflecting a new and different person.

The great happiness principle behind the Beatitudes is simple. It comes to light as Jesus begins to state conditions under which the ideally happy person lives. In the first Beatitude, Jesus does not say, "Blessed is the man with money in the bank." He says, "Blessed are the poor in spirit." The principle, then, is that we are happy because of *what we are,* not because of *what we do or have.*

Put in language such as Jesus might use today, the first Beatitude can be written as follows: "Happy and content and full of the joy of living are the humble, for theirs is the kingdom of heaven."

Upon reaching this point in my analysis, I had begun to feel a bit smug (still another name for human pride). I was too sure of myself. I only had to define words and the Beatitudes would explain themselves, or so I thought.

Then came the phrase, "kingdom of heaven," and I was stuck again. This time, my dictionary might just as well have been a mail-order catalog. It was no help at all, because I was now facing an unsettled problem which has puzzled theologians for centuries.

I was tempted simply to tiptoe away quietly and forget the whole thing. I could not compete with the great scholars who have debated this issue. I could not expect to make an original contribution. I would probably be called shallow—or worse yet, a heretic. But in spite of these difficulties, I had to work out my own answer, based, I hoped, on meanings Jesus intended to convey.

Just what *did* Jesus mean by "kingdom of heaven"? Where is heaven anyway? And when do we go there? These additional questions made me realize my ideas of heaven were indeed hazy. I had been told in Sunday school that heaven is a place in the sky where streets are paved with gold; where gates, guarded by angels, are of mother of pearl. I had also been told that after my death I would somehow arrive at those pearly gates; that after certain formalities, my name (in a huge book) would probably be checked off; that if I made this final hurdle, I could then enter in peace.

I had long ago discarded this picture of heaven, but had never replaced it with another. I certainly had spent enough time in church. Yet I could not remember ever having heard a simple explanation that satisfied my skeptical mind. I thought surely that such an explanation was possible. But where was I to look?

As I turned to the Gospels for help, I discovered still another problem: Is there any difference between "kingdom of heaven" (used twenty-three times by Matthew and not at all by the other writers) and "kingdom of God" (used three times by Matthew, ten times by Luke, twice by John, and seven times by Mark)?

I suppose I could have tarried over this problem—but as I have already indicated, I do not have a theological mind. I was thus willing to accept an uncomplicated answer. I based this answer upon the fact that Luke, in his version of the Beatitudes, says: "Blessed be ye poor: for yours is the kingdom of *God*" (6:20). I cannot explain why Matthew alone refers to "kingdom of heaven," but I believe that "kingdom of God" implies essentially the same meaning.

The remaining questions, however, were not as easily settled. The Beatitudes themselves simply do not tell us all we need to know.

I thus began to ask if Jesus anywhere mentions *when* the kingdom of heaven is supposed to arrive. I found that he does, in several places. Matthew, for instance, indicates that this is the main theme of Jesus' preaching. He writes: "From that time Jesus began to preach, and to say, Repent: for the kingdom of heaven is at hand." (4:17) In addition, Mark quotes Jesus as saying: "The time is fulfilled, and the kingdom of God is at hand." (1:15)

Furthermore Jesus does not say anything about having to die in order to enter the kingdom of heaven. He does refer to eternal life, but when he speaks of the kingdom of heaven, he says it is "at hand."

Jesus is asked by the Pharisees when the kingdom of God will come. He answers, "The kingdom of God cometh not with observation." (Luke 17:20) In other words, we cannot see it, hear it, smell it, or taste it. We cannot *sense* it. But, says Jesus, the kingdom is at hand. Now! And before the Pharisees can ask the next question, "Where?" Jesus answers all in the same breath: "Neither shall they say, Lo here! or, lo there! for, behold, the kingdom of God is *within* you." (Luke 17:21)

If we are to find the kingdom of heaven, then, we should look for it in our own hearts, now. It is not an experience in the remote past or in the distant future. It is now. This is the golden moment.

Several of the parables begin with the words: "The kingdom of heaven is likened unto. . . ." In a parable reported by each of the first three Gospel writers, the kingdom is likened unto a mustard seed, tiny now, but becoming a full tree when it is properly planted, watered, and nurtured. This is a way of indicating the importance of man's relationship with man and with God. When Jesus says a man shall find the kingdom of heaven, he is saying that man shall discover this relationship.

Theologians may complicate the matter. But I was sure that Jesus meant to state a simple truth that has to do with the present. I was sure Jesus spoke a simple language his uneducated audience could understand.

The first Beatitude might now be paraphrased as follows: Happy and content and full of the joy of living are the humble, for they live every day, here and now, and they have found the proper relationship between themselves and God.

My analysis of this Beatitude made more sense to me than anything I had ever heard before, in or out of church. I now began to see a glimmer of the light that Jesus brings to man.

CHAPTER TWO

They That Mourn

"Blessed are they that mourn; for they shall be comforted."

This is step two in the pursuit of happiness. Jesus has just told us that the first step toward a full and complete life is to learn how to be humble. In the next sentence, he tells us that happy are those who mourn, for they shall be comforted. This sounds like a paradox and it posed a lot more questions. Happy are those who mourn—those who are unhappy. How can that be? Who are the mourners and why are they mourning? What are they crying about?

Are they the folks who have suffered losses of possessions—money, a house that has burned, a stolen car, a torn dress? Is Jesus saying that if they mourn long enough and loud enough their losses will be restored?

Are these mourners the people who have lost a loved one—a son, daughter, mother, or father? Are they mourning because of failure? Have they lost a football game or a political race? Or have they failed to make the social register?

Perhaps Jesus is talking about the sinner who is mourning because of his wrongdoing and who is seeking forgiveness—like David in one of his songs. "Hear my prayer, O Lord, and give ear unto my cry."

Perhaps Jesus is talking about chronic pessimists who cry about everything: jobs, weather, traffic, politics, meals, relations or he may be saying that no matter what a person cries about his desires will be granted? That he will find happiness and contentment and that his problems will be solved, just because he has soaked them in tears.

I knew this was not true. I had never seen tears bring such results, and I had seen a few tears in my day, too. The truth is, I had shed a few myself.

I remembered one of my childhood sorrows. The time I threw my rubber ball into the creek and it floated away. There was nobody near to retrieve it. You have never heard such crying. But I never saw my brand new ball again.

No, mourning does not restore losses, does not *cause* good things to happen. If mourning did work that way, the New York Stock Exchange would never dip. And few persons would ever die, because mourners could extend life indefinitely.

No, Jesus is not talking about a way man can control the will of God. While it is true that the Beatitudes are keys to a superior kind of happiness, they are not guarantees against sorrow. Jesus urges us to pursue happiness. He points the way. But, at the same time, he warns that we will encounter sorrow. Mourning itself is not the key to glorious living. It is simply one of the facts of life we might as well accept.

When Jesus says that those who mourn will be comforted, he speaks like the wise father who finds his little boy crying over a lost ball. He does not replace the ball immediately. He tells his son not to worry, that things are going to be all right. He suggests a ride to the grocery store for Mama, takes the little fellow by the hand, walks with him to the car. By the time they have backed out of the driveway, the boy has stopped crying and is talking about something else. He regrets his loss, but more important things soon fill his busy head and crowd out his sorrows.

Jesus is telling us to expect sorrow but not to worry, that our mourning is only temporary.

Theologians may say I have missed Jesus' full depth of meaning here, that his message is not that simple, that I should stick to my own business. But to such imagined criticisms I can only reply that I believe the truth of the matter *is* simple. My attitude is like that of the blind man whom Jesus healed. The Gospel of John reports that when some church officials questioned this man, he could only reply: "One thing I know, that, whereas I was blind, now I see."

There must be some explanation.

Jesus has given us the first rule: Be humble. Now he hastens to tell us that happiness requires more than humility. He says that humility is the first step, but that there will be rough spots. He gives us his personal assurance that we will manage, that we will come out all right, and that in the end we will be comforted.

This Beatitude is not a rule by itself. Jesus is talking to those who already know about rule one, not to late arrivals who missed the first part of the sermon.

Jesus is not talking to the *rich* in spirit, to the man

whose barns have burned, or to the lamenting Wall Street speculator. Jesus offers no comfort to the lady left out of the social register—because when such a lady begins to live by rule number one, she can't care less. She finds something much more serious in life about which to mourn.

Jesus, then, is talking to the person who is already trying to practice humility. But even as the fullness of this meaning began to dawn on me, one question still hung on. Why? Why is sorrow necessary? If God wants us to be happy, why does he allow us to be sad? Why didn't he rule out the possibility of sorrow from our mental and emotional make-up?

It didn't take me long to see the fallacy in this line of questioning: for if God had made us insensitive to suffering, he would have made us something less than human.

What species would we be if we could see a child hit by a car and not rush to his aid? What normal person among us would not show emotion? The emotion of sorrow within the human breast is necessary. If we could not feel sorrow, we could not feel happiness. We would be less "human," as a matter of fact, than wild animals.

Let us watch the mother who meets her son at the bus station. He is coming home from college for the Christmas vacation:

She arrives at 4:20. The bus is not due until 4:42. To her, the dismal station is a bright foyer. She is not discouraged by the haggard and sleepy-looking travelers, by the confusion, or by the bus station smell. Everything is good today.

"Which ramp will it come in on?"

"Eight or nine, lady. Whichever is open. It will be announced."

"On time?"

"We don't know, lady. We don't get reports unless they are late. They usually run on time."

"Is that it?"

"No, it really isn't due yet. They never come *ahead* of time."

"Oh, there it is. No, that one is coming from the south. His will come from the north."

The bus finally arrives.

"Hold back the tears," she whispers to herself. "Where is he? He surely would have phoned if . . . oh, there he is. Hold back the tears."

She doesn't see anyone else. Just the boy. She does not notice the sailor with his awkward bag; or the old lady walking with a cane and carrying a box tied with string; or the young mother between two toddlers, and an infant asleep in her arms. She sees only her son. And the tears come anyway.

They are tears of joy, spring fed from her very heart. Forgotten now is the bleak day last fall when the bus station was dull and dark, the day her heart was mangled in every grinding gear. Her son's bus had arrived and departed much too soon that day because it carried him away to school. It was a slowly moving prison and her boy was its captive.

The tears that day were streams of grief. But now, they are tears of joy. This is a moment to cherish. A golden moment to keep locked in a jewel box, to fondle and enjoy on days when loneliness again returns to haunt her empty house.

Without the sadness of the parting there could be no joy in the returning. Without the one there could not be the other. That is what Jesus is saying. Blessed are they that mourn, who know the sadness of the parting, for they shall be comforted. They shall have the joy of the returning. For their hearts shall someday overflow and pound and burst with reds and yellows and the sounds of symphonies yet unwritten.

Yet, is this the final answer? Are we *supposed* to feel pain and misery? I believe that these further questions can be answered only in terms of faith in the mystery of God.

The mystery of innocent suffering remains unsolved. It is good that men are sensitive enough to weep, because insensitivity to suffering implies inability to have real joy. But men still ask how to do away with suffering, and they face a perplexing question. Job faced such a question, and instead of a detailed explanation, he received an affirmation that God is God and that man is man. The lesson is: While we should be sensitive to suffering, we should also take comfort in the mystery that God is God, and have faith that those who mourn will be comforted.

We can take comfort in the fact that Jesus also mourned. He knew the same anguish and sorrow that we must know if we are sensitive to the universe. We are following the example of Jesus when we mourn over tragic situations. But some situations, such as the lady who did not make the social register, are not really tragic. The only tragic element in such situations is that they reveal misplaced values and misspent efforts.

Jesus wept over the misspent efforts of man. He wept over the sins of the world. He wept for his fellow men, for you and me. He felt the discords that tear men apart, that imprison their minds and make them think only of self. He mourned for the self-centered, the self-righteous, the self-satisfied.

On the other hand Jesus points the road to happiness

and gives us the spiritual rules that can guide our paths. He says, in effect: "Blessed are they that mourn—they that mourn *when it is time to mourn*—for they shall be comforted."

With such assurance, a man can do great things. He can walk the road to happiness and a more abundant life without discouragement, without fear of defeat, without looking back. Nothing can stop his forward march.

Having found such assurance, I no longer seek a world filled only with sunshine. There is plenty of sunshine on the Sahara—a constant sun, with no rain, yet without rain there could be no fullness to the earth. Without rain the world would be out of balance.

So it is with the soul of man. Without the depth of feeling that allows us to know pain and sorrow and sadness, there would be no fullness to our lives.

Listen then once more to the words of Jesus: "Blessed are they that mourn, for they shall be comforted."

CHAPTER THREE

The Meek

"Blessed are the meek; for they shall inherit the earth."

This is probably the least understood of the Beatitudes, and perhaps the hardest to fit into place.

I hesitated a bit when I began to study this Beatitude. I was tempted to pass on to the next one, because at first glance, "meekness" doesn't quite ring true.

Meekness does not seem like a necessary ingredient in happiness, unless, of course, a person enjoys being pushed around. What normal person really wants to be meek?

There is a well-known comic symbol who personifies the American attitude toward meekness. His name is Mr. Milquetoast. Jokesters have kidded about him for years. They usually picture him as henpecked, spineless, and subservient, the brunt of pranks and foul deeds. Mr. Milquetoast has a wormlike backbone and a jellyfish constitution.

Our country was made great by men with get-up-and-go, and being a Milquetoast is the opposite of everything we have been taught to aim for. Without push, drive, or ambition, he is the man with the original hangdog look.

It is hard to imagine anybody *wanting* to be like him.

Yet, Jesus says, "Blessed are the meek . . ." Happy and content and full of the ecstasy of living are the meek.

I simply could not make myself believe this. I could not believe that a man with Jesus' understanding of human nature would stand before an audience and say that a fellow like that is happy, that meekness is a necessary condition of a more abundant life. I could not believe it. I did not want to believe it.

I picked up my dictionary again and found the words, "patient, mild, not inclined to anger or resentment." Then some secondary definitions, such as, "tamely submissive, easily imposed on, too submissive, spineless, spiritless." These definitions covered too much territory and obscured the meaning I was looking for. In addition, humility was listed as a synonym for meekness. Jesus certainly did not mean humility, because he had already talked about that.

I was not satisfied with any of these meanings, even though I did note one clue at the bottom of the entry, two obsolete usages: "gentle," and "kind."

I wondered if these meanings really were outdated. After all, my Bible had been translated in 1611. Were these meanings obsolete then? Were there other meanings during the days of Jesus? It occurred to me that if some meanings have become outdated in recent times, it is reasonable to suppose that still others existed in Old Testament days.

The place to check on this was the Bible itself, not the dictionary. So once more I laid Mr. Webster aside, and soon discovered that this Beatitude does not express a brand new idea. Actually, Jesus is quoting from the Old Testament. "But the meek shall inherit the earth" is found in Psalm 37:11, and is credited to David.

The real clue, then, is the Old Testament. Jesus is quoting David, a man who lived three thousand years ago. The word "meek" is also found in other places. In Numbers 12:3, for instance, I discovered that "Moses was very meek." As a matter of fact, Moses is described as meek "above all the men which were upon the face of the earth."

Moses—meek? The man who got so angry he killed a Pharaoh guard? The man so incensed at the treatment of the Hebrews that he organized his people and led them out of Egypt? The man who was their strong leader for forty years? The man who forged them into a nation?

According to modern ideas of the word, Moses was anything but meek. He was one of the most dynamic characters ever to march across the pages of history. When we think of Moses, we think of leadership. He was a man, not a Milquetoast.

If *Moses* was meek, modern definitions simply do not apply in his case. Meekness, in Moses, must have meant strength, not weakness—a special kind of strength, worth finding out about. I began to think this third Beatitude might be worth looking into after all.

I asked myself, "What kind of man, then, was Moses? Which of the words in the dictionary describe him best?"

"Was he patient?" Yes, he was. He had to be. He organized an enslaved and leaderless people into a powerful nation. He developed a group of nomads into a unity with character and a sense of purpose. He encountered their hostile attitudes and faced them toward their God. He was their ruler and judge for forty years, their source of assurance. And all this took patience.

Other usages of "meekness" had to be scratched from the list. Moses was certainly not easily imposed on, spine-

34

less, spiritless. Those are the Milquetoast characteristics that the word implies. But Moses wasn't like that at all. Then there are the two obsolete words, gentle and kind. Actually, these are the meanings some scholars give to "meekness." The French, for instance, put their word for gentlemanly into this Beatitude. They say, "Blessed are the gentlemanly, for they shall inherit the earth."

Again, what about submissiveness? Was Moses submissive? This question seems to prompt a yes-and-no answer. Moses certainly was not submissive to the Pharaoh, and he was not submissive to the murmurings of his followers, otherwise he would never have left Egypt. Or at best, he would have been overthrown by his own people.

Moses *was* submissive to God. Except for an occasional inclination to argue with God, Moses was submissive. He tried at first to dodge the challenge of God's words, "Come now therefore, and I will send thee unto Pharaoh, that thou mayest bring forth my people the children of Israel out of Egypt." (Exodus 3:10) But in the end, he submitted.

When Moses submitted, he did it like a man, a *gentle*man. He was a gentleman of the Lord. He submitted wholeheartedly and let God dominate his thoughts and actions. God's way became his way. He put God's way ahead of his own ideas of how the job ought to be done. He submitted his will to the will of God. He submitted to the leadership of the Lord.

Moses was strong, not weak. He was a gentleman. Not a fancy Dan, but a gentleman in the true sense: a man who put others before himself. Follow him for forty years and you will see. Here is a man with great strength of character, the meekest man on earth.

35

Thus Jesus says: "Blessed are the meek." Be like Moses "and you shall inherit the earth." Jesus also says: "Take my yoke upon you, and learn of me; for I am meek and lowly in heart: and ye shall find rest unto your souls." (Matthew 11:29) Here, and only here, does Jesus describe himself as having a particular characteristic. He says that he is meek, and that those who submit to his teachings shall inherit the earth.

Now comes the second part of the third Beatitude. What does Jesus mean by "inherit the earth"?

Inheritance is something we receive as a gift, a legacy, or a bequest. We do not *earn* an inheritance. It is given to us. Thus Jesus is not saying that if we practice meekness, we will earn the earth. He says that if we are meek, we will be *given* the earth. A significant difference.

Yes, but what do we get when we inherit the earth? A deed to something? All of the earth? If so, only one meek man at a time can inherit the earth. That is hardly what Jesus is talking about.

A more convincing meaning is illustrated by the man who "has it made," the man about whom it is said, "Things are rolling his way." Or perhaps you have heard that somebody "has the world by the tail on a down-hill drag." Such statements, divested of their economic implications, illustrate what Jesus means by inheriting the earth.

The meek man, in other words, will get everything there is to get out of life. He will enjoy the fullness of the earth. He will not be given wealth or a painless existence. But by submitting his will to the Lord, he is in command of every situation. He is not jealous. He does not seek luxury just because somebody else has it. He is not envious. He does not covet another's position, power, prestige, or status.

Such things simply do not enter his head. Rather, he is positive. He controls his own desires, is well adjusted, and his very being is guided by the will of God.

Yes, such a man "has it made," but not necessarily in a material way. He has it made because he has attained inner peace. He is slow to anger. He seldom gets burned up over life's obstacles. He rarely loses his temper in traffic, and never tells off the boss or fumes about circumstances beyond his control.

The meek man gets the most out of life because he gets the most out of himself. More than that, he gets the most out of his fellow man. Because he wants nothing that any man has, he can enjoy every triumph that comes into his neighbor's life: a special award, a raise in pay, a new baby. Whatever his fellow men get, the meek man is truly overjoyed because they have received it. A man with such a simple outlook finds plenty in life to be excited about, every day. He has no trouble finding happiness and abundant living.

Meekness, then, is really strength. It works for individuals and it *can* work for nations. It is a strength illustrated by Moses rather than by Hitler. While tyrannies do rise, we can take some comfort in the fact that they also fall.

"Blessed are the meek, for they shall inherit the earth." What an earth this would be if every nation were to take this Beatitude seriously! But such a thing, obviously, will not happen tomorrow. In the meantime, we must accept this great Beatitude as individuals, let it work in our daily lives, and hope that our example will spread to the nations.

CHAPTER FOUR

Hunger and Thirst

*"Blessed are they which do hunger and thirst
after righteousness: for they shall be filled."*

Jesus could have said: "Blessed are they that want to do good." This phrase conveys essentially the same meaning, but it lacks force.

One of the first things I noticed in my search for answers was Jesus' ability to use vivid language. The pictures he paints stand out because they are real and unforgettable. Even after many centuries, Jesus has great human-interest appeal, and we do not have to understand abstract terms to know what he is talking about.

Jesus said: "Blessed are they which do *hunger* and *thirst*. . ." These words were real to his audience, and they are real to most of the world today.

Jesus is not referring to temporary hunger. Not the hunger of a growing child who plays so hard he forgets to eat. Not the hunger of a working man who sits down to a full table. He is referring to permanent hunger, undernourishment from birth until death.

I am told that very few persons suffering from hunger actually starve to death. But they are so weakened by continuous undernourishment that they fall easy victim to common diseases. Most of the world's inhabitants are in this category. Most of the world's inhabitants suffer an acute and permanent hunger which few Americans have ever known.

Most Americans know pangs of prolonged hunger only when they decide to lose some weight. In the face of what I know to be true about the misery of other peoples, I reluctantly mention my own reducing diet. But I did lose twenty pounds, and this is the nearest I have ever come to understanding the constant hunger referred to by Jesus.

Even though my hunger was temporary, it was prolonged, and it was painful. I would be working at my desk when slow hunger would begin to gnaw inside. I would drink a glass of special diet liquid but without much relief. I would get up, walk to the kitchen, open the refrigerator, and just stare inside. I would look at the bread and butter and cheese and sliced meats, and leftovers from a meal I had not been allowed to eat.

It was pure torture. There were times when I could not get food off my mind. And in the end I cheated a little. I would take some crackers and cheese, add a slice of cold meat, wash the whole thing down with a soft drink, and then cut off a tiny piece of cake for dessert.

I found it impossible to resist the demands of hunger. When we get hungry enough, we forget everything else and think only of something to eat. Yet this illustration is inadequate. I experienced hunger all right, but it was only temporary. I did not really face the problem of permanent hunger. Think of what it means not to have a refrigerator door to open. Think of what it means not to be able to cheat a little on a diet.

There is a great difference, then, between temporary and permanent hunger—and those persons in Jesus' audience undoubtedly knew the permanent type. They lived in a desolate and impoverished back country dominated by Rome. They knew exactly what kind of hunger Jesus was talking about.

Jesus' hearers also knew thirst. They lived on the edge of the Arabian Desert and they had experienced thirst. They knew that thirst is, in a way, worse than hunger. A man can live quite a long time without food, but caught without water on a desert, he can perish in a day. They knew there is no such thing as permanent thirst.

Jesus, then, used language his hearers could understand. They knew hunger and thirst—and they could easily appreciate the idea of having these cravings satisfied. But they also knew that such satisfaction is only temporary. Hunger and thirst are urgent calls. They are never-ending. And such is Jesus' call for righteousness.

A man seeking righteousness is like a hungry man, a man who opens the refrigerator door and can't close it. A man seeking righteousness is like a thirsty man, a man whose parched throat craves the cool spring. A man can seek food and drink in vain, but when he seeks righteousness with deep and permanent cravings, he is bound to be satisfied. Nothing can stop him.

Such a man will seek righteousness every day—not just three times a day either, but all of every day.

Yes, that is how we should seek righteousness.

What is this thing that Jesus calls "righteousness"? He talks about it all through his preaching.

In trying to answer this question, I looked again at the

Old Testament—and found that "righteousness" is not a new word with Jesus. David sang about righteousness. In his first Psalm he sang: "For the LORD knoweth the way of the righteous: but the way of the ungodly shall perish." He closed still another psalm with these words: "For thou, LORD, wilt bless the righteous; with favour wilt thou compass him as with a shield." (Psalm 5)

Solomon also wrote about righteousness. In Proverbs 15:9 we find: "The way of the wicked is an abomination unto the LORD; but he loveth him that followeth after righteousness."

Psalms and Proverbs were written a thousand years before Jesus showed people the true relationship between themselves and God. In those early days the word meant to live right. A man who lived right was a righteous man. It was that simple.

It was that simple except for one question. What did right living mean to the Hebrews? And how did Jesus change this meaning?

I remembered the word, "meek." It was once strong, but it has become weaker through the centuries. The opposite is true of "righteousness." It was once weak, but Jesus gave it a stronger meaning.

What, then, did being "right" mean to the Hebrews of Jesus' day? The scribes and Pharisees could answer this question quickly. They thought being right meant following the law. They were legalists, and during the time of Jesus, this view dominated religious thought. The legalistic view, in simple language, is that to follow the law literally is to live right. The person who follows the law is righteous.

Jesus changed this idea at the very beginning of his ministry. In Matthew 5:20, we find: "For I say unto you,

That except your righteousness shall exceed the righteousness of the scribes and Pharisees, ye shall in no case enter the kingdom of heaven."

It was this new interpretation that got Jesus into trouble. These were strong words indeed. If I had been a Pharisee, I, too, would have been upset. Here I am, a Pharisee, an elder in my church. And this street-corner preacher has the nerve to tell my people that our ideas of right and wrong are not good enough.

If an evangelist came to town and spoke like this to a huge crowd in the city park or at the local armory, if such a man said that no Baptist, Presbyterian, or Methodist could enter the kingdom of heaven, it would cause a great commotion.

If something like this should happen on a national television hook-up, every special-interest group in the United States would issue a statement. The renegade preacher would be denounced. Somebody would start a movement. They might even try to pass a law to keep him out of public halls. Somebody, without a doubt, would want him run out of the country.

Jesus caused this kind of reaction. It was his reinterpretation of the law that sparked the opposition. He was a threat to the organized religion of his day, and he had to be silenced.

Thus, Jesus says it simply is not good enough to live by the letter of the law. A man can live by the letter of the law, exactly as the Pharisees advocated, and remain unrighteous. The Pharisees taught that if people followed the laws rigorously (more than six hundred of them), they were on solid ground.

Jesus says we must *think right to be right*. We can't think wrong and live right. For example, we are right in condemning murder, but we should also condemn the evil thought within us that leads to murder. The evil thought, not the deed itself, is the root of the matter.

Right at the beginning, Jesus gives a new meaning to the word, "righteousness." He improves the word, spreads it out, gives it a new dimension. And while this interpretation does away with legalism, it actually requires more than the Pharisees demanded. It is much harder to eliminate the thought than it is the deed.

Righteousness means more than just being right in following a specific law. Righteousness refers to a person's total outlook, his disposition, the tone of his life.

Modern dictionaries reflect this new meaning. To be righteous is to act in a just, upright manner. Righteousness is further defined as doing what is right; virtuous; morally right or justifiable. A synonym is the word, "moral."

The sum of Jesus' teaching is often said to be the golden rule: "Do unto others as ye would have them do unto you." The golden rule is an example of right living, above and beyond legalistic requirements.

In his fourth Beatitude, Jesus tells us that happiness and contentment and the fullness of living will come to the man seeking the right way of life; seeking with the same burning desire that the hungry man craves a meal or that the thirsty man anticipates a cool drink of water.

If a man searches for the right way of living in that manner, he shall be filled with understanding.

Such an understanding (of right thinking and living) will not come to the man who "can take it or leave it." It will not come to the man who says to himself, "It is there in the Bible on my living room table—and one of these days, when I get time, I intend to read about it. I

43

just don't have time right now because my favorite television program is just coming on."

No, the understanding that Jesus is talking about will come to the man who craves it, who is hungry for it.

In the opening words of Psalm 42, David says: "As the hart panteth after the water brooks, so panteth my soul after thee, O God."

A thousand years later, Jesus, standing on the mountainside in Galilee, said: "Blessed are they which do hunger and thirst after righteousness: for they shall be filled."

CHAPTER FIVE

The Merciful

"Blessed are the merciful; for they shall obtain mercy."

Jesus is saying here that the man who shows mercy to other men takes still another step toward a fuller and more abundant life. At first glance, this Beatitude causes no trouble. It seems simple and easy to understand.

Almost everybody believes in mercy. Most persons would probably rate themselves as merciful human beings. Some of the other Beatitudes might be hard to live by, but not the one about mercy. After all, there's the Salvation Army, the United Fund, and the Goodwill. Yes, we understand about mercy. We give to the poor. We give to various drives to promote better health. We spread mercy around freely. Our mercy is well organized too.

As a matter of fact, we don't even give mercy a second thought—and this, of course, is the trouble. Mercy is not something to be "dispensed" at regular intervals. It is not balancing financial records for tax purposes or ridding closets of last year's clothes. It is not something we do as a matter of course. Mercy has a more inclusive meaning.

As Jesus expands Hebrew law to include how a person feels in his heart, he also makes mercy something greater than a few benevolent acts. He does this type of thing in all the Beatitudes. He gives big ideas, each of which implies a number of others. For instance, he does not name loyalty, fairness, courage, wisdom, or temperance. But his big ideas cover these attributes, and others too.

So it is with the fifth Beatitude. It covers more than appears on the surface.

A classic description of justice and mercy appears in Shakespeare's *Merchant of Venice*. Portia, speaking to Shylock, says:

> The quality of mercy is not strain'd,
> It droppeth as the gentle rain from heaven
> Upon the place beneath. It is twice bless'd:
> It blesseth him that gives and him that takes.
>
> . . . .
>
> It is an attribute to God himself;
> And earthly power doth then show likest God's,
> When mercy seasons justice.

Six hundred years before Jesus preached the Sermon on the Mount, Micah also talked about justice and mercy. He said: "and what doth the LORD require of thee, but to do justly, and to love mercy, and to walk humbly with thy God?"

Webster defines mercy as: "refraining from harming or punishing offenders, enemies, persons in one's power; kindness in excess of what may be expected or demanded by fairness; forbearance and compassion; a disposition to forgive, pity, or be kind; kind or compassionate treatment; relief of suffering."

And Jesus says: "Blessed are the merciful." Blessed are those who show mercy because mercy shall be shown to them. We shall be shown kindness in excess of what may be expected or demanded by fairness if we have shown this type of consideration to other persons.

Mercy, then, goes beyond ordinary expectation. To be merciful we must go beyond. We must walk the extra mile. Jesus is saying that we must exceed the day-to-day standards of fairness. He could have said, "Blessed are the just and the fair-minded." But, he goes further than this. He says, "Blessed are the merciful." Mercy includes justice, but mercy is justice with something else added.

Mercy also depends upon justice, because we must be in a position of judgment before we can show mercy. A boy at school breaks a rule. The principal must judge his action. He can be severe *or* lenient without showing mercy at all—if he does not first study the case and make a fair judgment. Mercy comes into the picture only after a fair judgment has been made. Then, and only then, can the principal show mercy, if he is so inclined.

Mercy, then, should be distinguished from pity, compassion, sympathy, or some other emotion. We can feel these emotions toward a person in trouble, but they do not necessarily imply mercy. We can be merciful only when we sit in judgment and have the power to act.

We may pity a friend who can't pay his debt to the bank. But we can't be merciful to him, because only the banker can extend his loan. And before the banker can show mercy, he must understand our friend's problem. He must also be disposed (within legal requirements) to forgive our friend's record. He must show forbearance, kindness, and consideration.

47

Or, consider the case of the chicken thief. It is winter and he is out of work. His family is starving. He was driven to his act by poverty and necessity. We understand his plight. We pity him and his family. We feel compassion for him. We feel he should be forgiven. We feel he should be shown mercy. But, there is nothing we can do about it, because the chickens he stole belonged to somebody else.

We can show him mercy only when he steals *our* chickens. And that's a different set of chickens entirely. It is much harder to show mercy when our own chickens are involved.

Take another case: A man borrows his brother-in-law's lawn mower. He uses it all afternoon and leaves it beside his garage. It rains. The owner happens to drive by his house and sees the mower getting wet. Right then, he forms a judgment. Never again will he lend him anything.

Next day, the mower is still there. It stays out in the weather for a week. When it is used again, a blade is broken. The owner finally retrieves the remnants, only to discover the thing won't run at all. His brother-in-law has forgotten to mix oil with the gasoline.

The brother-in-law is a bit sheepish about all of this, and says he will pay the damages. The man takes the mower to the shop, tells the repairman to fix it, that somebody else is footing the bill, that he wants the mower made like new. "Don't *repair* it. Put in all new works. Yes, including a new blade. Let's teach him a *good* lesson."

Now this is where justice, understanding, forgiveness, forbearance, and *mercy* come in:

When the brother-in-law finally offers to pay up, the owner tells him to forget the whole thing. Not only that, he lets him borrow it again when the weeds at his place have grown up. He even helps him lift the mower into his station wagon.

That's being merciful. I doubt that I could do it. It isn't easy. There are times, of course, when justice must be done. Nevertheless, mercy is an act of the will. It does not *excuse*, it forgives—and we cannot forgive and still hold a grudge.

Mercy, then, is a step beyond justice, fairness, compassion, and forgiveness. These things come first. Then mercy is the crowning achievement. It is the gracious, sympathetic, and understanding act that exceeds what is fair and expected.

Thus, Jesus teaches his disciples to pray: "forgive us our trespasses as we forgive those who trespass against us." And on the mountainside, he says: "Happy is the man who shows mercy, because in the end he shall be shown mercy."

Just what is it that comes into the life of a person who shows mercy? How are the merciful made happy? How does being merciful help develop a richer and more abundant life?

The man who cleanses himself of bitterness and resentment and revengeful thoughts against his fellow man is well on the way to the full life. He is richer than the man whose days are spent thinking of ways to get even with his neighbor; or in fuming over lawn mowers and brothers-in-law.

The man who can understand an offense, put it in the proper perspective, and then temper justice with mercy is the sort of fellow who has peace of mind.

Resentment breeds resentment; worry breeds worry; distrust breeds distrust. By the same token smiles breed smiles, good will breeds good will; friendliness breeds friendliness.

The same is true of mercy: Happy and content and full of the joys of life are those who know how to be merciful, because in the end, mercy will be reflected back into their own lives.

Mercy breeds mercy. Jesus says so.

CHAPTER SIX

The Pure in Heart

"Blessed are the pure in heart: for they shall see God."

I wondered about the pure in heart. This Beatitude is surely out of reach—beyond the capabilities of average fellows. When Jesus speaks of the pure in heart, does he mean *absolutely* pure in heart, sinless? Does pure in heart mean morally perfect?

Nobody I know of is perfect. I certainly am not. Jesus must mean something else. Otherwise, the Beatitudes, as practical rules, break down at this point. And we no longer need eight Beatitudes. One is sufficient, and it can read like this: "Blessed are those who are perfect, because they shall have everything."

Such a Beatitude, however, helps me very little in my search because man has too many trials, troubles, frustrations, worries, anxieties, labors, sorrows, and discouragements. I cannot be helped by well-meant advice to be perfect. Such counsel is like telling an injured person to stop bleeding.

Jesus does not preach that kind of message. His listeners are ordinary people with ordinary dreams, desires, and problems. Jesus is giving them advice that they can understand—and follow.

Looking back again into the Old Testament, I found that Jesus' idea of a pure heart is not new either. In Psalm 24, I found these words: "Who shall ascend into the hill of the LORD? or who shall stand in his holy place? He that hath clean hands and a pure heart."

Jesus, of course, is referring to a spiritual quality when he uses the term "heart." By *pure* in heart did he mean a spiritual heart cleansed of impurities? Yes, but what impurities do we find in our hearts? Or what impurities do we recognize in the hearts of our neighbors?

I can make a long list: despair, ugliness, dejection, suspicion, hypocrisy, jealousy, intemperance, envy, greed, selfishness, revenge, vanity, pride, conceit, discourtesy, hate.

Any one of these impurities can generate enough spiritual and mental poison to make a person—and all his associates—miserable. Any one of these evils can destroy hope for a fuller and better life. In order to find the full life, then, we must cleanse our hearts of such basic evils.

Can anyone be happy if his heart is filled with suspicion and jealousy? Or can a man experience the ecstasy that comes with a new day if he thinks always of himself, or if his heart is filled with despair?

Jesus tells us to cleanse our hearts, to purify our emotional life, to get rid of our misery-producing thoughts, to throw out our mental trash.

Of course there is only one way to do this. We must fill our hearts with the rich and exciting emotions that bring happiness. We can't just remove the bad. We must replace the bad with something good. Otherwise, we are like the man who cuts weeds without planting anything in their place. The result is an empty backyard. In order to make the space beautiful or useful, he must plant something good in it, perhaps flowers or vegetables.

We cannot cleanse our hearts of the evil, time-wasting, misery-producing emotions unless we replace them with something which is healthy, positive, and happiness-producing.

If we are interested in developing a pure heart, then let us make a written list of the evil in our mental attic. We must also list the good qualities we would have there instead. Seeing such things in writing helps us analyze ourselves and self-analysis is a step toward developing the pure heart Jesus advocates.

Here is a start: Do we suffer periods of despair? If so, let us write this down. Then, opposite this entry, we will write the everlasting symbol of Jesus' teaching, the word "hope."

The first step in building a clean heart is hope. We must somehow turn our despair into hope.

Here are some other suggestions, just as important. We must change ugliness into beauty; dejection into cheerfulness; suspicion into trust; hypocrisy into sincerity; jealousy into understanding; intemperance into temperance; enmity into friendliness; selfishness into self-denial; revenge into forgiveness; vanity into modesty; conceit into meekness; discourtesy into courtesy; pride into humility; hatred into love.

Each one must make his own list. Then he can do some spiritual house cleaning. He won't end up perfect. Nobody is perfect. But he will be on his way, and this is what matters.

Happy and content and full of the richness of life is

the man with the clean heart—the man who is free from the emotional trash of the world—for he shall see God.

How do we *see* God?

Jesus, of course, is not talking about optics. He refers here to spiritual sight. This Beatitude is Jesus' rule for acquiring insight. When Jesus says we will see God, he means we can learn the true nature of our relationship with God. God and heaven are here now, in the world about us, every day. The kingdom of heaven is at hand— within us, now.

Jesus, then, is saying that the man with a pure heart, a heart uncluttered by evil thoughts, will have the spiritual perception necessary to see what is going on around him. He will be able to see God in his daily heaven. He will be able to find himself—*and* God.

To see God is to see truth, and Jesus says when we find the truth, the truth will make us free. The man who finds the truth will find the full meaning of life, its full possibilities, its bounties, its blessings.

It is easy to see that a man who harbors jealousy, hate, greed, envy, bitterness, and other impediments, cannot see God. Such a man is just not in tune with God. He cannot see the truth.

It is clear now what Jesus is talking about. The man with the clean heart, the man with a heart filled with the highest emotions, is well on the road to finding truth.

When he finds truth, he finds God.

Yes, he finds God. He sees God. He sees God a thousand times a day. He sees God first in the early morning in the bright yellows and thunderous reds of the dawn; he sees God directing the universe. He also sees God in the smile of a friend, in mother love, and in a thousand other ways.

Only the man with the pure heart can see such things. The man with a curse on his lips and hatred in his heart is barred from full appreciation of the abundant life.

No man is perfect. But all men can move in the direction of the perfect. And, blessed are those who aim in this direction, for they shall see God.

CHAPTER SEVEN

The Peacemakers

*"Blessed are the peacemakers; for they shall
be called the children of God."*

In analyzing this Beatitude, I noticed
a slight change of pace. Up to this point, Jesus has been
talking about general attributes. Now he is more specific.
The peacemakers are in a class by themselves. They are
singled out and the rule is definite. Jesus wants us to be
peacemakers, and his meaning is clear.

My first thought was that Jesus saved the easy one
until almost last. It is a natural. I'm not mad at anybody.
Everybody yearns to live in a peaceful world, so we might
as well go on to the next Beatitude.

But wait. Jesus is not saying that the man who merely
wants peace is blessed. He is not referring to the peaceable
man who does not fight with his neighbor.

Jesus' listeners would certainly have voted for peace.
And if we should name our greatest desire as a nation,
most of us would undoubtedly say, "Peace." If asked to
explain, we might say something like this: "The threat
of war is the greatest problem in the world today. Once

we solve this problem permanently, we can manage other human problems with ease."

Jesus knows his listeners prefer peace to war. But blessedness does not come to those who merely dream of a day when "they shall beat their swords into plowshares, and their spears into pruninghooks," a day when "nation shall not lift up sword against nation," or "learn war any more." Isaiah expressed man's longing for peace well—and succeeding generations have appreciated his words.

Jesus is not talking about the longing for peace which we all feel. He is talking about peace*making,* and this calls for action. Jesus wants us to do something for him. He wants us to make peace. He wants us to undertake "operation peacemaker."

Such an operation is complicated—especially if we think of it as the overall program necessary to promote world peace. We all agree that action is necessary. But what is the first move? How do we get potential enemies to go along with *our way* of thinking? How do we get them to calm down and live right?

There are no simple answers to the over-all problem. But, at the same time, we must remember that Jesus is giving practical advice to individual persons. I do not believe his Beatitude about peacemaking implies an over-all program. World peace should certainly be our goal, but we must begin with particulars rather than with a general plan of action.

Then where *do* we start?

I believe the first step toward peace is a step toward God. Before we can move in any other direction, we must make peace with the Almighty.

Imagined voices now ask me what this means. "Is man at war with God? Surely not." But I believe that he is, and I also believe that this war is our basic problem.

Jesus tells us, for instance, that the world is divided into two camps. We are either for him or against him. We cannot serve on both sides. We serve God when we obey his rules, when we live according to his wishes. This means replacing self-centeredness with outgoing thoughts about mankind. Then, and only then, are we on the Lord's side.

Many of us try to serve in the army of God. We try. We work at it for awhile until he sends us on a difficult mission, one that eats into our bridge-playing time. Then, some of us desert to the enemy. We indulge in the slip-shod practices that are momentarily attractive. At these times we are on the side of the world.

We still claim to believe in the golden rule and all of that. But we also argue for practicality. After all, this is the modern age, a complex age of overlapping values. We are living in America, a complex society. The golden rule is all right until we get in that morning line of traffic. After all, how long would it take to get to work if we didn't fight the traffic?

We argue for the golden rule except when it comes to the matter of stretching income-tax deductions. After all, if we didn't do this, the government would take everything. The golden rule simply does not apply during the first week of April.

The fact remains that we cannot live at peace with God if we are going to work for him on a part-time basis. He does not want week-end soldiers. He wants full-time regulars.

Let's make peace with God. And when we do, we must surrender.

Let's surrender our lives to God. Let's seek him out

at his headquarters and say, "We submit our wills to yours." Let us go to him in meekness. Let us make our peace with him.

This is a move we simply must make. Jesus says, "Blessed are the peacemakers," not, "Blessed are those who are willing to live in the peace that someone else establishes." The first step in the process is submission. "Come unto me all ye who are weary and heavy laden and I will give you rest."

Once we make peace with God, the next step is easy because we now have God on our side. Without his help, we cannot take the second step, because the second step is to make peace within ourselves.

What does it mean to make peace within myself? Surely I am not fighting myself. I believe that any person who will sit and study about this idea for a little while will finally conclude that he is his own worst enemy.

Let us add this up and give ourselves an honest answer. How much of the misery and unhappiness in life can we lay directly at the door of somebody else?

Let us think for a minute. Our neighbor didn't intend to make us unhappy. He may have said something that hurt our feelings, our pride. But, if we didn't have tender feelings in the first place, if we had not been thinking of ourselves and our own little world, his words would have gone in one ear and out the other. We would not even have noticed them.

Maybe we feel neglected—neglected by parents, by husband, by friend. (Blame it on somebody.) The fact remains, however, that if our thoughts were not self-centered, we could not possibly experience the feeling of neglect.

How do we start making peace with ourselves? How

do we develop an outlook that results in peace of mind? Here is a suggested exercise. It isn't easy. I find that it is sometimes embarrassing. But whenever I can muster up nerve enough to practice it, I always feel immediate results:

We must look in the mirror; look ourselves straight in the eye. Then we will ask ourselves this question; "Have I made peace with God? Am I at peace with myself?" We must do this the first thing every morning.

We will ask ourselves about peace of mind. We will tell ourselves that this day, just today, we are going to make peace with ourselves. And somehow, this little trick works. It works because it helps us analyze ourselves.

The idea is not new. I once met a man whose firm depends on orders placed by phone. Disturbed by a decline in business, he studied the conversations of his employees, and soon realized they just didn't sound friendly. As part of a training program to develop better phone personalities, he mounted a mirror beside each desk in his office. Thereafter, employees answering the phone found themselves staring at their own images. This changed their way of talking. When we look ourselves in the face, it is almost impossible to be insincere.

It is as Polonius told his son: "To thine own self be true, and it follows as the night the day, thou canst not then be false to any man."

The role of the peacemaker, of course, is not as easy as it sounds. But once we have made peace with God and ourselves, we are ready to take the third step. We can start making peace with our fellow men. If we are not really fighting anybody, we are to be congratulated. If we are, we had better get to work.

What about the fellow whose name was left off the

list this year? What list? Any list. Maybe the committee didn't ask his help or advice when he thought they should have. So what did he do? He began to ignore the project. He says he isn't exactly opposed to it, but that he just doesn't work for it any more.

What about the acquaintance who says a few things that have got back to us? Oh, we speak when we have to, but we don't go out of our way any more.

Most personal battles center around hurt feelings—pride. About 87½% of them anyway. We must make a truce, surrender our pride.

We must set out to repair the leaks in our dikes of friendship. There may not be many, but they must be repaired. We can call that friend we haven't spoken to since her husband burned a hole in our carpet. We can go to see that fellow who forgot to invite us to the Christmas party. It is very necessary that we keep our friendships in good repair.

At this point in "operation peacemaker," we begin to discover that by making peace we have found peace. If we have done a creditable job, our reward will be to realize about now what Jesus meant by the "peace that passes all understanding."

At this point, another type of question pops up. Now that we are such good peacemakers, we might wonder how to make peace between Charlie and Helen. Or how to unify the PTA. Or what to do about international peace. Isn't that what a peacemaker is supposed to do, make peace all around?

These are very good questions, but answers to them are difficult. We might be able to do something for Charlie or Helen, *if* they should seek our advice, but chances are we could not accomplish much simply by giving them advice, by preaching to them. Assuming we are asked to help, we might accomplish something by listening. They might learn something from us, but ultimately they must make their own peace with each other.

The PTA is a little different. We can do something, assuming we are a participating member. We can set a good example, refuse to talk about either side, suggest creative projects to promote unity. But in the long run, the factions will have to reconcile themselves to each other, and no group ever exists in perfect harmony with itself.

The international problem is much more complex. Because in this case we cannot avoid being part of a faction, even if we do not serve in the armies or work in an agency. We are beset with the gnawing problem of what we, as good Americans, can do. And the more we know about decisions in government, the more we realize the immense complexities involved in trying to do the right things as a nation.

Governments face very real and dangerous problems. Complex problems, to be sure, but not altogether unsolvable—for to a degree at least the world is the individual person multiplied many times. This means that each person must do what he can. But each person must begin as a human being. Some make high level decisions; but even they are "human," and should begin, as private citizens, to be peacemakers on very personal and practical levels.

Jesus is giving advice and comfort to the private citizen. His Beatitude about the peacemakers is obviously related to international conditions—and these concern us all. But the main task is to spread peace through the example of our personal lives—in the faith that peace breeds peace.

We must do what we can, and in principle, this Beatitude ultimately solves world problems.

The ultimate solution is beyond us at the moment. We can only say that we are in the hands of God. We can only submit to him, make peace with ourselves, with our neighbors, and then do what we can—in faith—for the world at large. We can only know one thing for sure about peace, and that is what we learn from personal experience: Operation peacemaker can work *now* in the lives of individual persons.

"Blessed are the peacemakers, for they shall be called the children of God."

CHAPTER EIGHT

The Persecuted

"Blessed are they which are persecuted for righteousness' sake: for theirs is the kingdom of heaven.

Blessed are ye, when men shall revile you, and persecute you, and shall say all manner of evil against you falsely, for my sake.

Rejoice, and be exceeding glad: for great is your reward in heaven: for so persecuted they the prophets which were before you."

As we read this final Beatitude, we may find it a bit hard to believe. Similar to what Jesus says in the second Beatitude, "Happy are they that mourn," he is saying here, "Happy is the man who is persecuted."

In the first seven Beatitudes, Jesus lists attributes of character that go to make up the ideal man. As a windup, he tells us what to expect if we are successful in aiming toward this ideal.

We would expect a person with such fine Christian qualities to be embraced by everybody, welcomed in any company. If we were planning a public-relations campaign for a young politician, we might tell our candidate to develop the stimulating qualities suggested in the Beatitudes. We might say to him, "Live that kind of life and everybody will like you. That is the way to win friends and influence the voters."

But Jesus warns his audience not to expect a friendly response from everybody. He tells them they can expect to be persecuted.

There are, of course, many types of persecution. Among the best known are persecutions for racial, political, and religious reasons. Strong convictions invite persecution.

We can even be persecuted because of the friends we keep or the way we dress. I can think of nothing worse than being persecuted by the gossip of neighbors in a small town. This would make me miserable from morning till night.

The final Beatitude, then, is hard to understand. To me, persecution has always meant the opposite of happiness. Yet Jesus says that happiness and contentment and the joy of living will come to the man who is persecuted.

Of course, Jesus qualifies this statement. He adds: "for righteousness' sake," and "for my sake." He could have said: "Happy is the man who is persecuted for thinking and living right—and for following me and my teachings." Jesus assures us that such a man will discover the kingdom of heaven. The man who is persecuted for righteousness' sake, like the man who learns true humility, finds fullness of life or the kingdom of heaven.

Jesus does not say that the genuine Christian is universally unpopular. But he does say that a man who lives as a Christian will surely attract some opposition.

Why are those who try to live right sometimes persecuted? And how can persecution help lead to a full and joyous life?

The supreme illustration of being persecuted for righteousness' sake is Jesus himself. He lived according to his Beatitudes. He lived the perfect life but he did not please everybody. He stirred up opposition so fierce that it cost his life.

Of course, the persecution of Jesus took place some two thousand years ago; if he were in the United States today, he would not be crucified. The mob would not actually kill Jesus today, but they might put him behind bars for being subversive.

Why does goodness or right living stimulate opposition?

One reason some folks are persecuted is because they desert the crowd and go their own ways. Their convictions do not allow them to follow the popular trend. This is a common reason for persecutions.

Here is an illustration: A young girl joins her pals who sneak cigarettes after school. But she refuses to participate in the fun. When asked why, she says, "I just don't believe it is right." She is sometimes respected for this, but not always. She may be teased and nagged, called a goody-goody—and if she persists in not being one of the gang, she may suffer isolation, the worst penalty of all.

Persecution of this type may seem unimportant. But the young lady in question has a real cross to bear. All because she tries to do what she believes is right. Standing outside the crowd, she risks being persecuted for righteousness' sake.

Persecutions are not confined to teen-agers: For instance, during a convention of salesmen the men decide to visit the girlie show. One of the men declines. The others resent this, because his high standards are unspoken criticisms of their actions and they feel guilty.

Because men are bound to justify their own actions (even when they feel guilty about them), the persecution begins. It begins with talk. Nothing violent of course. Just talk. And many of the remarks are prefaced by the familiar phrase: "Now don't get me wrong, I really like Charlie, but. . . ." Then they really let him have it.

Their talk covers everything about the man. Not just his staying behind at the hotel. They remember another time when he suggested having an annual banquet without the usual hospitality hour. They also recall other ways in which he has been a prude. They conclude that he just isn't the right "type" of person. When it comes time to elect a president, Charlie is not even considered, mainly because he is a wet blanket. His unpopular stand may also cost him business.

Why? Because an upright action silently vetoes actions not based on the highest ideals, and people do not like to be made uncomfortable. An upright action also generates envy among those unable to stick by their own moral guns. The result, naturally, is opposition.

There is another reason for opposition to the genuine Christian, and this is the basic cause of Jesus' death: The man who stands up for what is right—*and speaks out about it*—is a disturbing element in the community. He threatens to upset the local apple cart.

He is called, among other things, a crank, crackpot, fanatic, fool, do-gooder, narrow-minded reformer, misguided intellectual. Such labels are placed upon any man who has the courage of his convictions.

67

Anyone who does not believe that the courageous Christian is so persecuted can perform a simple experiment: Let him hire a hall and make some prohibition speeches. His cause will be unpopular, and he will find this out quickly, because people will laugh at him. Or he can go to Mississippi and talk in favor of integration. His cause will again meet opposition, this time of a less jovial nature.

Jesus says that being persecuted for trying to do what is right leads to a fuller and more abundant life. The final Beatitude thus tells us to do what is right, regardless of consequences. This Beatitude challenges us to stand up and be counted.

We should, of course, avoid the martyr complex; we should not *enjoy* being persecuted. We should not, without good reason, upset people on purpose. Jesus says, "Blessed are they which are persecuted for *righteousness'* sake." He does not say that suffering is a good thing, or that suffering in and of itself is a sign of right living.

Suffering is suffering. It is not an automatic sign that we are right. Further: Just because we think we are right does not mean that we *are* right. We can be wrong. One of the greatest misfortunes in the world is enthusiastic ignorance, working ourselves to death going in the wrong direction. We may be sincere, yes, but sincerely ignorant.

The key to this Beatitude, then, is the *why* of the persecution. Not everybody who is persecuted is right. Jesus attaches the qualifying phrases: "for righteousness' sake," and "for my sake." Only the persecuted who meet these qualifications can expect to find happiness.

Before claiming that our persecutions result from our being right, we must evaluate ourselves. Perhaps Jesus put this Beatitude at the end so that we might use the other seven as a check list.

Let us check ourselves to see if we are poor in spirit, if we are really humble. As we go down the list, we may find we no longer feel persecuted about petty things. This is a good sign, because it means we are learning to live above false values. If we measure up, we are bound to feel some *real* opposition, and this is a sign that we are beginning to arrive.

Why is this?

To begin with, it isn't the persecution that brings happiness. Persecution is nothing more than an indication of what is happening. Persecution is a kind of measuring stick. Maybe social scientists should invent a new term here, something like "persecution ratio."

Here is how the persecution ratio works. If we are being persecuted because we are living right—according to the check list—we can rest assured that we are fighting on the Lord's team. We have arrived. Jesus says we are in good company. He says that if we work so hard at being a Christian that we are beginning to attract opposition, then we are in the same company with the prophets. We are also in the company of Jesus.

We are fighting in the right army. We are not fighting everybody. We have more friends than enemies. And when we see who our enemies are, we should be comforted.

Being persecuted also means spiritual growth. Nobody ever became an athlete by watching television. We develop through exercise. Physical *and* spiritual. When we battle for the sake of righteousness, we profit more than anybody else. We develop our own spiritual powers. We become stronger persons. This spiritual strength leads to a fuller and more abundant life.

If we really want to raise our persecution ratio, we must work hard at what is right, and the opposition itself will lead us to a higher usefulness. We will then be worth something in the army of Jesus.

The final Beatitude, then, is a call for work. It is not a rosy promise. Jesus is perfectly frank. He says in substance, "Follow me. The road is rough, but it is well worth taking."

A Spiritual Inventory

There they are—the Beatitudes, the key to the richest treasure in the world.

Eight spiritual laws. Eight statements of truth that can open the door to the full meaning of life for each of us *if* we take time to think about them, to study them, to apply them to our daily lives.

They will work if we learn to use them.

I speak from experience. Since discovering this key, I have stepped into a new world of living.

I do not mean that I have learned to live one hundred percent by the Beatitudes. This is a big order. To live one hundred percent by the spiritual laws of Jesus implies perfection, and I have never found a perfect person.

These spiritual laws give me a *guide* to follow—a goal to aim for. They help me understand where I am going. They give me purpose. A sense of direction. They give me insight into myself and my neighbors, and help me understand the world.

These simple rules have changed my life. People say they see the difference. I can certainly feel the difference from inside.

There are no more days I can't handle, no more problems that overwhelm me. I have forgotten my despair and depression. I believe I have seen the last of gloom and despondency.

If Jesus were on earth today, he would probably repeat these spiritual laws. They are as true now as when he uttered them on that desolate hill in Galilee. Their basic meaning has not changed.

There would be only one difference. Jesus would speak in modern language, in terms we might more readily understand. His illustrations would be about the everyday people of the twentieth century.

To get the most out of the Beatitudes and to make them easier to understand, I have translated them as best I can into the words of my own vocabulary.

They have become an inventory sheet in my life, a list of my basic needs, and I use them as a daily check list. I hope my readers will try it. This is how to do it:

First, write down the Beatitudes the way they appear in the Bible. Then write below each of them—in familiar words—what they mean to you.

Second, use these statements as a checklist. Check yourself. See what spiritual items are missing from your inventory, then stock up your personal warehouse with the proper qualities.

Here is how I carried out this exercise:

1. Jesus says: "Blessed are the poor in spirit; for theirs is the kingdom of heaven."

Today he might say: "The humble man with a contrite heart is full of happiness and contentment and the ecstasy of living, because he has come to himself, has experienced a new birth of spirit, and has found his true relationship with God and his fellow man."

Then I ask myself if I fit into this category. Do I have a sufficient supply of humility on hand? Do I approach each day with a contrite heart? Am I unobtrusive as I go about my work, as I contribute my labors to my church, as I enter into the activities of my community?

Do I experience the happiness that comes to the man who demands nothing—who expects nothing? To the man who stands at the beginning of each day in the presence of God and is thankful just for being here? To the man who does not think he *deserves* certain material benefits or honors or courtesies or considerations, who is not after a lot of publicity, who does not want a brass band to meet him at the station?

If so, I have begun to learn what Jesus is talking about. I will see good about me everywhere: in the smell of fresh-cut grass, in the dazzling bright of the snow-covered hills, in the deep green of trees in a park, in the wave of your neighbor's hand, and even in the smile of a bus driver.

Everything has a new meaning. Each day will bring something new.

When I approach the day with humility, I start from the beginning, with nothing. Anything that comes along is better than what I started with. I don't expect great things, so even little things are exciting.

In order to reach this state of mind, my first job is to purge myself of the desire for glory. This is a hard thing to do.

For instance, I still find myself expecting and enjoying flowery introductions when I speak at dinner parties. Praise feeds my ego. It lifts me up in the clouds. There isn't too much wrong with this, except for one thing: I sometimes expect praise which the toastmaster forgets to give. And I feel let down, I feel unhappy. Yes sir. I think to myself: What a lousy dinner! What a dumb toastmaster! What an evening wasted!

If I can just keep from expecting praise, everything works out fine, even if the toastmaster does forget what he was going to say. On such occasions I am genuinely surprised by gracious words of introduction, and these are the golden moments. If these words do not come, however, I do not miss them.

In order to get more out of every moment of life, then, I must approach the day with humility. This is the first step in the pursuit of happiness.

2. "Blessed are they that mourn; for they shall be comforted."

Jesus might have said it like this today: "The high emotion of happiness can be appreciated only by someone who understands the deep emotion of sadness; who understands that there is a time to mourn and a time to laugh. Such folks find comfort and joy, and recognize moments of happiness when they arrive."

Now I check myself again. Are the sorrows in my life the kind of sorrows that prepare me for happier moments, or are they sorrows that lead only to further sadness and further misery?

The secret here lies in the *reasons* for my sadness. Frustrated personal desires lead only to bitter tears. Concern for others helps develop rich emotion. Without the valleys of sadness there can be no hills of joy.

I must understand the place of sorrow and sadness in my life. I must learn that there is a time to mourn and a time to laugh. Then I will have taken another step toward the full and happy life.

Jesus says we will have sadness, but that in the end, our days will come out all right.

3. The third checkpoint concerns meekness. Jesus says: "Blessed are the meek; for they shall inherit the earth."

If he were speaking today, Jesus might point out that the word "meek" has undergone a change in meaning during the past two thousand years. It has become a weaker word. He might explain how Moses exemplifies the real meaning of meekness. He would surely repeat his statement: "I, too, am meek and lowly in heart and if you will listen to my teachings and learn of me and take up my yoke and follow me, you will find rest unto your souls."

Jesus might explain the quality of meekness in this manner: "Learn to submit yourself—in all you do and in all you think—to the will of God. And when you do, you will find the fullness of life. You will then be able to say, 'The world is mine.' "

4. Next comes a question of degree. Jesus says: "Blessed are they which do hunger and thirst after righteousness: for they shall be filled."

Now I ask myself: "How hard am I working on my inventory? How hard am I working to find the right answers? How eager am I to follow the right way?" This is my fourth checkpoint.

Am I hungry? Am I searching for the right way of life like a man who thirsts for water on a sun-scorched desert?

Or have I acclimated myself to the world of material pleasures? Has my search for the fuller and richer life been diverted? Have I become a spiritual slob? If so, I will never reach the end of my search.

If I really want the answers to life, I must search for them as Jesus suggests. Happy is the man who—with drive and determination—seeks the right way of living, for he will surely find it, and his hunger and thirst will be satisfied.

5. I stop for a long time at this checkpoint as Jesus says: "Blessed are the merciful; for they shall obtain mercy."

This Beatitude demands real soul-searching. Do I show true mercy to my fellow wanderer when it is my lot to judge him? Do I render judgments of my neighbors in accordance with the golden rule? Or do I talk about fairness, justice, and mercy when I am only a bystander?

Have I learned to go beyond what is expected of me in fairness? Have I learned to forgive and forget?

I take time to check myself on this one. I think about it. I remember that Jesus says if I learn the true meaning of compassion and forgiveness; if I learn to render the deeds of mercy by going beyond the requirements of justice and fair play, I will find that the world will return to me a fair share of mercy.

6. As I check myself against the first five Beatitudes, I stop now to see if I have given myself truthful

answers. I am honest with myself, because Jesus says, "Blessed are the pure in heart; for they shall see God." In other words, I must seek the full life with personal integrity.

I ask myself whether or not I have cleansed my heart of evil thoughts. Have I purged myself of ugliness, dejection, suspicion, hypocrisy, jealousy, intemperance, enmity, selfishness, revenge, vanity, conceit, discourtesy, pride, hatred?

Have I filled my heart instead with beauty, cheerfulness, trust, sincerity, understanding, temperance, friendliness, self-denial, forgiveness, modesty, meekness, courtesy, humility, love?

The test gets more difficult as it goes along. But I feel that if I pass this checkpoint safely, I will find happiness, because Jesus says that the person who has purified his heart—who has purged it of evil and filled it with good—will have found God. Such a person will be able to see God in everything he thinks and sees and does.

7. Now I come to the point where I can feel results, where I can discover how my spiritual inventory is shaping up.

I must have done well up to this point because I begin to feel it deep inside.

Jesus says next: "Blessed are the peacemakers; for they shall be called the children of God."

Jesus isn't talking about the peace lover, or the person who votes for peace and says, "Peace is wonderful." The peacemakers must also act. They must *do* something. They must make peace, not simply enjoy peace when and if it should arrive.

I ask myself, "Have I made peace?"

I resolve to do so—to make peace with God, with myself, and then with my fellow man. The success of my task will be complete only when I can say I have found the peace that passes all understanding.

And when that great day comes, God can look upon me and say, "This is one of my children with whom I am well pleased."

8. The final checkpoint! "Blessed are they which are persecuted for righteousness' sake; for their's is the kingdom of heaven. Blessed are ye, when men shall revile you, and persecute you, and shall say all manner of evil against you falsely, for my sake."

I feel that if I can pass this one reasonably well, I will have arrived. I wouldn't get this far, I know, unless I made good marks on my previous lessons.

It is now time to graduate, so I give myself this final test. I ask myself bluntly: "Am I working so hard at being a Christian and showing others the way and talking about it so much that I am running into some opposition? Opposition from within myself, wanting to follow my old ways of living; opposition from my friends who think I am being stuffy; opposition from the community in which I live because I swim against the crowd and dare to fight against the evils of society?"

If I can stand up straight and give an affirmative answer to this final question, I can step up and receive my diploma. I have made the grade.

I am in good company, too. Jesus himself says so: "Rejoice," he says, "and be exceeding glad; for great is your reward in heaven; for so persecuted they the prophets which were before you." They are indeed exclusive company.

There they are, the great rules of life, the qualities that make up a full life, the guideposts leading out of darkness into the brilliance of a new day.

These guideposts will open up a new world for everyone who follows them.

I know. They have opened up a new world for me.